Royal Wedding

Prince Harry and Meghan Markle

By Conrad Jarrett

ISBN: 978-1-387-45305-4

According to Meghan it was "Just a cosy night ... we were just roasting chicken... just an amazing surprise, it was so sweet and natural and very romantic. He got on one knee."

This is the love story of Prince Harry and American actress Meghan Markle. How they met, their courtship, his proposal, and the royal wedding.

Dedicated to my mother for encouraging me.

All photographs contained in this book are "Labeled for Reuse" on Google Images and are either in the public domain or labeled as Creative Commons.

No images of either Prince Harry or Meghan Markle are used.

Table of Contents

Once upon a time … a handsome English prince met a beautiful American actress

Their Story

On May 19, 2018 at St George's Chapel at Windsor Castle in Prince Harry of the United Kingdom will marry the American actress Meghan Markle. This is the story of who they are, their wedding, and how they met.

How they met

Britain's Prince Harry first met actress Meghan Markle in Toronto, Canada in early 2016, having been set up on a date by a mutual acquaintance. That friend is believed to be Markus Anderson, a Canadian consultant for the Soho House Group and a former global membership director at the exclusive club, and one of Meghan's "closest friends in the world". Markus is understood to have set up a date between the television star, who was 35 at the time, and Prince Harry, which whom he is also on friendly terms. Markus Anderson has been part of Meghan's inner circle for a number of years and has several photos with her on social media.

That first date was set up sometime in the spring of 2016, and Meghan and Harry are believed to have carried on their trans-Atlantic love affair for several months after Harry bombarded her with texts. By June of that same year love had blossomed into a committed relationship. By

October, the two were being seen together publicly.

It's Official – They're in a Relationship

Their relationship was first acknowledged on November eighth 2016 when an official statement was released from the royal family's communications secretary addressing the "wave of abuse and harassment" directed toward Markle that followed the announcement of her relationship with Prince Harry.

How Prince Harry Proposed

According to Meghan it was "Just a cosy night … we were just roasting chicken… just an amazing surprise, it was so sweet and natural and very romantic. He got on one knee."

The engagement ring he gave her consists of three diamonds, two of which were taken from the jewelry collection of his mother, Diana, Princess of Wales.

Official Word of Engagement

Their engagement had been officially announced by the royal family on November 27th, 2017. The following day the date and place of the wedding was announced as May of the following year at Windsor Castle. Since then a lot has been written about the social significance of Meghan being a royal proud of her mixed-race heritage.

Love

Wedding

Windsor Castle, May 19, 2018 …

Prince Harry sits at the altar of St George's Chapel waiting for his American fiancé. Meghan is wearing the engagement ring he gave her, consisting of three diamonds, two of which were taken from the jewelry collection of his mother, Diana, Princess of Wales. Soon they will both be wearing wedding bands, because this is their wedding day.

Markle is the second American, and only the first person of mixed race heritage, to marry into the British royal family.

Cost

Experts believe the wedding will cost around half a million pounds, or about 650 thousand American Dollars. The royal family is paying for the wedding out of its own treasury. No public dollars will be used, nor does the British government plan to make the wedding day a bank holiday (as was done for the wedding of Prince William and Catherine Middleton).

Title

It has been speculated that Prince Harry will be created Duke of Sussex and Meghan will then become Her Royal Highness the Duchess of Sussex after the wedding.

The Groom – A Short Biography of Prince Harry

Harry was born Henry Charles Albert David, the Prince of Wales on the 15th of September 1984. He is the younger son of Charles, the Prince of Wales, and Diana, the Princess of Wales. At the time of his birth he was third in line to the British throne, but with the birth of his older brother's two children (Prince George and Princess Charlotte) he has slipped to fifth in line.

Harry was educated at schools in the United Kingdom and spent parts of his gap year in Australia and Lesotho. He then chose a military career and underwent officer training at the Royal Military Academy Sandhurst. He was commissioned as a cornet (i.e. second lieutenant) into the Blues and Royals, serving temporarily with his brother, and completed his training as a troop leader.

In 2007 and 2008, he served for over ten weeks in Helmand, Afghanistan, but was pulled out after an Australian magazine revealed his presence there. He returned to Afghanistan for a twenty week deployment in 2012–13 with the Army Air Corps. He left the army in June 2015.

Harry launched the Invictus Games in 2014, and remains patron of its Foundation. He also gives patronage to several other organizations, including the HALO Trust, the London Marathon Charitable Trust, and Walking With The Wounded.

The Bride – A Biography of Meghan Markle

Meghan Markle is an American actress and humanitarian born in 1981 to a Caucasian father and an African-American mother. She is most famous for her portrayal of Rachel Zane in the television series “Suits” and in the role of Amy Jessup in the science fiction show “Fringe”. Today, however, she is best known as the future wife of Prince Harry.

Meghan is Born

"Meghan" was born as Rachel Meghan Markle on the fourth of August, 1981 in Los Angeles, California in the United States of America to Thomas Markle and Doria Ragland.

Thomas Markle is a Hollywood cinematographer, while Doria Ragland is a yoga instructor and psychotherapist who has a Master's of Social Work degree from the University of Southern California.

Parents

According to Meghan:

> "It was the late Seventies when my parents met, my dad was a lighting director for a

soap opera and my mom was a temp at the studio. I like to think he was drawn to her sweet eyes and her Afro, plus their shared love of antiques. Whatever it was, they married and had me. They moved into a house in The Valley in LA, to a neighborhood that was leafy and affordable. What it was not, however, was diverse. And there was my mom, caramel in complexion with her light-skinned baby in tow, being asked where my mother was since they assumed she was the nanny."

Home and School

So Meghan grew up in a suburb of Los Angeles, California. From the beginning, Meghan has always been educated in private schools. From the age of five she attended the Hollywood Little Red Schoolhouse, a primary school known for having a fabulous swimming pool and playground.

Later she graduated from the all girl's Immaculate Heart Roman Catholic High School, a college preparatory school in Los Feliz, California known for its beautiful campus in the Hollywood Hills. Among its alumni are super model Tyra Banks and actresses Mary Tyler Moore and Yara Shahidi.

In 2003 she graduated with a bachelor's degree in theatre studies and international studies from Northwestern University, a prestigious college located near Chicago.

As part of her studies she interned at the United States Embassy in Buenos Aires, Argentina.

Meghan's Adult Life

From September 10th, 2011 until their divorce in August of 2013, Meghan was married to producer Trevor Engelson. They had been in a relationship for seven years by the time they had married.

Until November of 2017 Meghan resided in an apartment in Toronto, Ontario, Canada; the location where the television show Suits was filmed. She has since moved out and has stated that she will not be appearing on the show anymore (see "Retirement" section).

Among her friends are Serena Williams, Ben Mulroney (son of the former Prime Minister of Canada, Brian Mulroney), and Ben's wife Jessica Mulroney.

Meghan has described herself publicly as a "foodie" and a "geek". She was an early investor in the Apache HTTP Server.

Work

Entertainment Industry

Meghan's father, Thomas Markle, worked on the set of the television series "Married… with Children" for many years, and he would often bring young Meghan with him. This exposed her to the entertainment industry from a young age.

In 2002, while still a student studying theatre at Northwestern University, Meghan appeared in an episode of the daytime soap opera General Hospital. Following that she appeared in two episodes of Season Two of the Fox television series Fringe as Junior Agent Amy Jessup.

Meghan is best known for her portrayal of Rachel Zane, a paralegal in the show Suits. The program is shown on the USA Network and filmed in Toronto, Ontario, Canada.

In addition to her television roles Meghan has also appeared in three feature films: Get Him to the Greek, and Remember Me, both released in 2010, and Horrible Bosses which was released in 2011.

Other work includes the short film The Candidate, and television episodes of The League, Castle,

Without a Trace, The War at Home, The Apostles, 90210, Century City, Love Inc and Cuts.

Television Work

Below is a partial list of Meghan's television appearances:

2002, Appeared for one episode as Jill in General Hospital

2004, Appeared as Natasha for one episode in Century City

2005, Appeared as Cori for one episode of "Cuts"

2005, One episode of "Love, Inc"

2006, Appeared in one episode of "The War at Home"

2006, Portrayed Veronica Perez in the episode "Murder Sings the Blues" of CSI: NY (season 3: episode 7)

2008, Meghan portrayed Wendy in the first episode of the first season of "90210"

2008, appeared in one episode of 'Til Death

2009, one episode of Knight Rider

2009, appeared in episode 15, season 7 of "Without a Trace"

2009, first episode of season 2 of "Fringe" (as FBI Agent Amy Jessup)

2010, in "CSI: Miami" Meghan appeared as Officer Leah Montoya in season 8, episode 20

2011–2017, in her most prominent role Meghan portrayed a regular main character, Rachel Zane, in "Suits".

2012, appeared in "Castle", season 4: episode 17.

2014 , Portrayed Amy Peterson in the Hallmark Channel television movie "When Sparks Fly".

2016, Portrayed Cassandra Brand in the Hallmark Channel television movie “Dater's Handbook”.

Film

Meghan has appeared in several feature films. In 2005 she appeared as a passenger on a plane in “A Lot Like Love”. In 2010 she had an uncredited role as Tatiana in “Get Him to the Greek”, and as Megan in “Remember Me”. The following year she portrayed Jamie in “Horrible Bosses”. Most recently she portrayed Kirsten in the film “Anti-Social”.

Calligraphy, Modeling, and Other Work

Meghan is an accomplished calligrapher and has used that skill to support herself during breaks in her early acting career. She has also done modeling and, for a time, was the television show Deal or No Deal as the "briefcase girl". She was also thc founder/editor of the defunct lifestyle website known as The Tig, and has released a line of clothing with the Canadian company Reitmans.

Humanitarian Work

Meghan credits her parents and her high school for starting her commitment to humanitarian work. Her alma mater, Immaculate Heart Roman Catholic High School, requires public service to graduate. She has carried this ethic throughout her life.

In 2016 Meghan traveled to Rwanda after she became a global ambassador for World Vision Canada. In that role she promotes the agency's Clean Water Campaign to assist third world nations in developing safe, clean drinking water.

Meghan has also worked with the United Nations to promote gender equality and women's empowerment. She has also worked with the charity One Young World, and spoke on gender equality and modern day slavery at their 2014 annual summit in Dublin, Ireland. She was also an attendee at their 2016 summit in Ottawa, Canada.

Race and Slavery

In 2015, in an article in Elle Magazine, Meghan wrote about her race and racial issues:

> “'What are you?' A question I get asked every week of my life, often every day. 'Well,' I say, as I begin the verbal dance I know all too well. 'I'm an actress, a writer, the Editor-in-Chief of my lifestyle brand The Tig, a pretty good cook and a firm believer in handwritten notes.' A mouthful, yes, but one that I feel paints a pretty solid picture of who I am. But here's what happens: they smile and nod politely, maybe even chuckle, before getting to their point, 'Right, but what are you? Where are your parents from?' I knew it was coming, I always do. While I could say Pennsylvania and Ohio, and continue this proverbial two-step, I instead give them what they're after: 'My dad is Caucasian and my mom is African American. *I'm half black and half white.*'

Writing about life as a biracial seven year old Meghan says

" I had been fawning over a boxed set of Barbie dolls. It was called The Heart Family and included a mom doll, a dad doll, and two children. This perfect nuclear family was only sold in sets of white dolls or black dolls. I don't remember coveting one over the other, I just wanted one. On Christmas morning, swathed in glitter-flecked wrapping paper, there I found my Heart Family: a black mom doll, a white dad doll, and a child in each color. My dad had taken the sets apart and customized my family."

As mentioned, Meghan Markle's father is Caucasian, while on her mother's side she is black, having descended from African's brought to America as slaves. Through her mother she is the great-great-great grand daughter of a slave on a Georgia plantation who was freed after the

American Civil War. In that same article in Elle Magazine, Meghan wrote of her slave ancestor:

> "in 1865 (which is so shatteringly recent), when slavery was abolished in the United States, former slaves had to choose a name. A surname, to be exact. Perhaps the closest thing to connecting me to my ever-complex family tree, my longing to know where I come from, and the commonality that links me to my bloodline, is the choice that my great-great-great grandfather made to start anew. He chose the last name Wisdom. He drew his own box."

Her mixed race has caused issues at times in her life. Writing about here difficulty finding work early in her career she wrote "I wasn't black enough for the black roles and I wasn't white enough for the white ones, leaving me somewhere in the middle as the ethnic chameleon who couldn't book a job."

Late in 2016 the Royal Family issued an official statement that addressed the "wave of abuse" directed at Meghan. The statement talked about racist and defamatory stories being written about her.

Meghan Meets a Prince

Meghan's relationship with Prince Harry, fifth in line to the British throne, began in June of 2016. In a story in the September 2017 issue of Vanity Fair Meghan talked about her love for Harry for the first time publicly "We're two people who are really happy and in love. We were very quietly dating for about six months before it became news, and I was working during that whole time, and the only thing that changed was people's perception."

The couple made their first official royal engagement appearances at the 2017 Invictis Games in Toronto, first at a tennis event, and then at the closing ceremonies.

After she had met the Queen several times, it was officially announced by the Royal Family that Meghan and Prince Harry had become engaged. It is expected that they will wed in early 2018.

The Bride's Family Tree

Here are the first four generations of Meghan Markle's family tree:

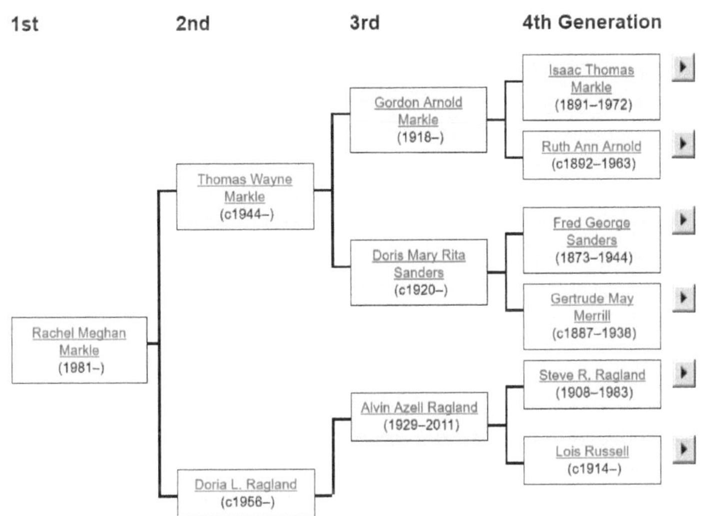

Father's Family Tree – British Nobility

Meghan's uncle, Mike Markle, determined that her father's family had roots in the royalty of Tudor England, having descended from Mary Hussey Smith, a New Hampshire landowner who died in 1908. Through her Meghan is descended from John Hussey, 1st Baron Hussey of Sleaford who was beheaded in 1537 by order of King Henry VIII of England. Along this line she is also a direct descendant of King John, the signer of the Magna Carta, who lived from 1166 to 1216.

Meghan is also a descendant of Christopher Hussey who was appointed the Governor of the Royal Province of Hampton (New Hampshire) in 1679. Christopher was also a Founding Father of Nantucket.

Blood Relationship with Prince Harry

It has been said that you look far enough back, everyone is related. For Meghan and Prince Harry, one only needs to look back four hundred years. Both are direct descendants of Elizabeth Bowes who died about 1572. They are thus, extremely distant cousins.

Twitter Reaction

Former U.S. President Barack Obama:

Michelle and I are delighted to congratulate Prince Harry and Meghan Markle on their engagement. We wish you a lifetime of joy and happiness together.

1:13 PM - 27 Nov 2017

Democratic Unionist Party leader Arlene Foster issued the following erroneous tweet:

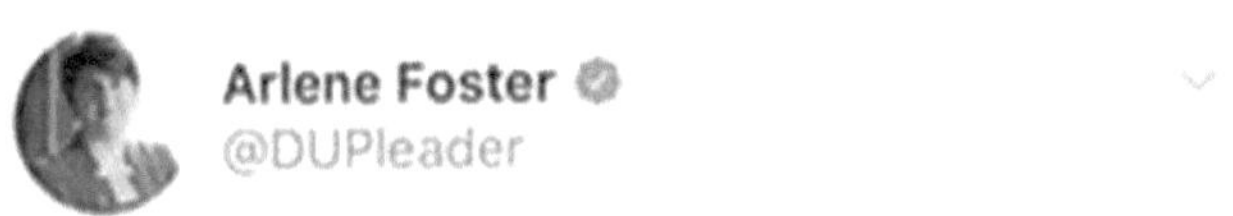

Congratulations to HRH Prince William on his engagement to Megan Markle. Wonderful news this morning!

Royal Wedding

Arlene quickly corrected her mistake:

Apologies to TRHs Princes William & Harry for tweet error on my account earlier. I stopped tweeting personally a long time ago. Genuine typo by a member of staff. Guilty of tweeting too fast. There goes any chance of an invite!! :-) AF

8:02 AM - 27 Nov 2017

Other tweeters were in a humorous mood:

Michael Chappell
@BlueLizardDes

#PrinceHarry very smart man, Planning wedding after #BlackFriday now he can always grab a bargain for anniversary's #royalwedding Happy days

5:46 AM - Nov 27, 2017

Life After Marriage

After the marriage Meghan and Harry are expected to reside at Nottingham Cottage, a royal residence in London on the grounds of Kensington Palace. She also intends to become a citizen of the United Kingdom.

Meghan stated during a BBC interview that she will not return to the television series Suits, and that she will transition out of acting work after the wedding. She is expected to devote her time to humanitarian causes.

Sources

Griffiths, Emmy (Nov. 27, 2017) “Prince Harry reveals how he proposed to Meghan Markle”, Hello Magazine

Boyle, Louise (Nov. 26, 2016) “A cozy lunch with the 'matchmaker' who is her closest friend - how Harry's girl Meghan Markle marked her 'romance' going public” - Daily Mail

Vonberg, Judith (Nov 29, 2017). “Meghan Markle intends to become UK citizen after marriage to Prince Harry”.

Markle, Meghan (July, 2015). "I'm More Than An 'Other'". Elle Magazine.

"Prince Harry and Meghan Markle: Seven Things We Learned About the Royal Couple". BBC. 27 November 2017.

"Prince Harry to marry Meghan Markle". The Guardian. November 27, 2017.

Griffiths, Emmy. "Will Meghan Markle use her first name Rachel if she marries Prince Harry?". Hello!. September 8, 2017.

"Meet Meghan Markle: Prince Harry's Feminist, Philanthropist, Actress Girlfriend". Vogue. November 18, 2016.

Blair, Olivia (October 31, 2016). "Who is Meghan Markle: The 'Suits' actress, humanitarian, activist and gender equality campaigner". The Independent.

Willgress, Lydia. "Who is Meghan Markle and how long has she been Prince Harry's girlfriend? Everything we know about the royal relationship". The Telegraph. September 22, 2017.

"The Duke of Cambridge approved Prince Harry's plea to trolls to leave Meghan Markle alone". The Telegraph..September 5, 2017.

Michael Holden; Guy Faulconbridge (November 27, 2017). "From blind date to Botswana's stars, Prince Harry charts love for U.S. actress Meghan Markle". Reuters.

Boyle, Danny (November 8, 2016). "Who is Meghan Markle? Everything we know about Prince Harry's girlfriend". The Daily Telegraph. London

Melas, Chloe (November 3, 2016). "Meghan Markle: 5 things to know Prince Harry's rumored love interest". CNN.

"Meghan Markle: Six things you didn't know about Prince Harry's girlfriend". The Week. November 8, 2016.

Dewan, Angela; Isaac, Lindsay (November 8, 2016). "Meghan Markle: Prince Harry warns press about harassing girlfriend". CNN.

Goulet, Matt (July 13, 2013). "Q&A:The Beautiful Meghan Markle on Suits, Canada Day, and Handwriting". Esquire.

Hicks, Tony (November 1, 2016). "Prince Harry ready to meet Meghan Markle's father". Mercury News.

Morris, Regan (September 26, 2017). "'Meghan who?' LA shrugs over Harry's hometown girlfriend". BBC.

Woustra, Kristy. "Who Is Meghan Markle: The Actress Was Changing The World At Age 11". Huffington Post. Canada. November 8, 2016.

Hodgkin, Emily (September 23, 2017). "Meghan Markle and Kate Middleton's path to royalty REVEALED – from Hollywood to Kensington". Daily Express. UK.

Midgley, Dominic (November 5, 2016). "Meghan Markle: The actress who made her mark on Harry". Daily Express.

Willgress, Lydia; Boyle, Danny (September 21, 2017). "Who is Meghan Markle? Everything we know about Prince Harry's girlfriend". The Daily Telegraph. January 7, 2017.

Kim, Jae-Ha (February 12, 2013). "Celebrity travel with Meghan Markle". Chicago Tribune.

"EXCLUSIVE: Harry's girl is (almost) straight outta Compton". Daily Mail. Australia. November 3, 2016.

Andreeva, Nellie (June 23, 2009). "Meghan Markle joins 'Fringe'". The Hollywood Reporter.

CNN, Judith Vonberg,. "Meghan Markle: Who is Prince Harry's bride-to-be?", November 27, 2017.

Hibberd, James (August 24, 2010). "Meghan Markle books lead role on 'Legal Mind'". The Hollywood Reporter.

Falzone, Diana. "Meghan Markle will quit acting following engagement to Prince Harry". Fox News. November 27, 2017.

"Experience the World of Suits Star Meghan Markle's New Lifestyle Site, The Tig". InStyle. December 20, 2016.

"As Meghan Markle Shuts Down Her Lifestyle Site, Source Says Speculation It's Related to Prince Harry Is 'False'". People. April 7, 2017.

Delap, Leanne (November 5, 2016). "Suits star Meghan Markle launches 'accessible' clothing line at Reitmans". Toronto Star.

Watkins, Janelle (February 29, 2016). "Meghan Markle 'Suits' Up for Success". Ebony.

Singh, Harmeet (August 7, 2015). "UN Women turn on the light". Strategy Online. Brunico Communications Ltd.

"Justin Trudeau welcomes Emma Watson, Bob Geldoff, and other star activists to Parliament Hill". Ottawa. ctvnews.ca. May 9, 2017.

"Hitched, Hatched, Hired". The Hollywood Reporter. September 27, 2011.

Vallance, Adam (November 8, 2016). "A Statement by the Communications Secretary to Prince Harry". The Royal Family.

Robert Booth and Lisa O'Carroll (November 8, 2016). "Prince Harry attacks press over 'wave of abuse' of girlfriend Meghan Markle". The Guardian.

The Sun (February 11, 2017). "Miss Meghan Markle – An Apology". The Sun.

Maria Puente (November 8, 2016). "Who would want to 'smear' Prince Harry's new girlfriend Meghan Markle?". USA Today.

"WTF? British Website Calls Prince Harry's Black Girlfriend 'Straight Outta Compton'". Black Entertainment Television. November 2, 2016.

"Meghan Markle, Wild About Harry!". Vanity Fair. September 5, 2017.

"Meghan Markle attends Invictus Games". BBC News. September 24, 2017.

"Prince Harry, Meghan Markle make first official public appearance". ABC News. September 26, 2017.

Bourke, Latika (November 27, 2017). "Royal wedding: Prince Harry and Meghan Markle announce engagement". The Age. Fairfax Media.

"Who put the sparkle on Markle? Five answers about the royal engagement - Macleans.ca". November 27, 2017.

"Inside Meghan Markle and Serena Williams' Friendship: Why She Credits the Tennis Star as Her Closest Friend and Confidante". E! News. April 9, 2017.

"How Meghan Markle and Princess Kate's Styles Differ — and How to Get Meghan's Best Looks". People. April 1, 2017.

"EXCLUSIVE: Inside Meghan Markle's Life in Toronto: From Prince Harry's Low-Key Visits to Cozy Yoga Classes". Etonline.com. December 15, 2016.

Furness, Hannah (November 19, 2017). "King Henry VIII ordered for Meghan Markle's ancestor to be beheaded". Daily Telegraph. UK.

Dean, Bailee (November 19, 2017). "Meghan Markle's ancestral tie to the Royal Family dates back centuries". News Limited.

"Prince Harry and Meghan Markle are actually cousins". Metro UK. October 30, 2017.

"Prince William Ancestry". FamousKin.com. 2017.

Magna Carta Ancestry: A Study in Colonial and Medieval Families, 2nd Edition. Douglas Richardson. 2011.

Markle, Meghan. "Meghan Markle: I'm More Than An 'Other'". 2017 Hearst Magazines UK (December 22, 2016) – Originally written in July 2015 published in ELLE Magazine in 2015.

About the Author

Conrad Jarrett is a freelance writer who lives near Seattle, Washington.

www.ingramcontent.com/pod-product-compliance
Ingram Content Group UK Ltd.
Pitfield, Milton Keynes, MK11 3LW, UK
UKHW041833200726
13854UKWH00003BA/1117

9 781387 453054